Books by Richard Tillinghast

Poetry

Sleep Watch
The Knife and Other Poems
Sewanee in Ruins
Our Flag Was Still There
The Stonecutter's Hand
Today in the Café Trieste
Six Mile Mountain
The New Life
Sewanee Poems
Selected Poems
Wayfaring Stranger
Blue If Only I Could Tell You
Night Train to Memphis

Translation

Dirty August: Selected Poems by Edip Cansever,
in collaboration with Julia Clare Tillinghast

Essays, Memoir, Literary Criticism & Travel

Robert Lowell's Life and Work: Damaged Grandeur
Poetry and What Is Real
Finding Ireland: A Poet's Explorations of Irish Literature and Culture
Istanbul: City of Forgetting and Remembering
Journeys Into the Mind of the World: A Book of Places

Night Train to Memphis

poems

Richard Tillinghast

WHITE PINE PRESS | BUFFALO, NEW YORK

White Pine Press
P.O. Box 236
Buffalo, NY 14201
www.whitepine.org

Publication of this book was supported by public funds from the New York State Council on the Arts, with the support of Governor Kathy Hochul and the New York State Legislature, a State Agency.

Acknowledgements: See page 79

Printed and bound in the United States of America.

ISBN 978-1-945680- 79-3

Library of Congress Control Number: 2024939688

Night Train to Memphis

For Joshua Tillinghast, first-born

the look on my son's face   a moment old

like the river   old like rain
older than anything that dies can be

Contents

I.

2.

Night Train to Memphis

3.

Cross the river
with me. Even if this time the waters
don't part before us. Even if this time God
doesn't come to our aid and a flurry of arrows
riddles our backs. Even if there is no river.

—Luis Alberto de Cuenca
(Gustavo Pérez Firmat translation)

I.

The Mission

I freed my greyhound from her collar,
whispered into her ear her mission—
then loosed her into the night to fleetfoot
under the moon, searching across the fields,
her paws imprinting the snow.

Beyond the frost on the window, the tick
of the clock, the volumes of Dickens on the shelf,
something out there was listening, I was sure of it.
I tapped the barometer, paced, fretted as I waited.
But I must have nodded, the fire was ashes
when her paw on the door woke me.

She was holding my word in the sly smile
of her mouth. She'd folded it in a leaf.
Menace bristled in that word.
Snow was sowing daggers in my garden.
I locked us inside and brought the fire to a blaze.

The Feast of the Hungry

Every window in the big house
blazed, brilliant with beeswax candles,
Murano chandeliers, torches
in sconces. Wayfarers across the snow,
their feet near to freezing,
peered through frozen branches
    at this festival of lights.

Hunger, misery, the cold in their
extremities, they fancied they could
smell—these wanderers—the pig
roasting on a spit over the fire—
hear the fiddle and psaltery, the rustle
of taffeta, the clacking of dancers' heels
    on the parquet floor.

The bloodhounds that might have been
whistled up to harry them
off the grounds
snored in the entrance hall,
having gnawed on bones
the wayfarers would have fallen on
    like dogs themselves.

Why am I telling you this? It's certain
that those at the top of fortune's wheel
will never tire of feasting and making merry.
As for the poor, they are as Jesus said
they always are. Our headlights illuminate them
along the garbage-strewn freeway
    in their tents and lean-tos.

Skylark

We treasure-hunted her
through every junkyard on the dusty fringes of
Oakland and San Francisco,
dreaming we would find her—
hood staved in, mice
nesting in her upholstery, eucalyptus
leaves ribboned along the sleek
lines of her fenders.

We were men who loved beauty,
Carlos and Billy and I.
And because we were American men,
we looked for beauty in an automobile.

A Buick Skylark, 1953—
light-wing'd dryad
of the open road, as Carlos called her,
riffing on Whitman and Keats,

like the song that was also Skylark.
Johnny Mercer and Hoagy Carmichael wrote it,
Ella Fitzgerald sang it.

While our wives and children slept,
we were going to work nights in Billy's garage
grinding the rust out,

smoothing and priming and painting her
to gleam like the sea off Laguna Beach.

Her half-life began
before Trump, before Q-Anon,
before Nixon, before McCarthy,
before J. Edgar
effing Hoover.

How brief her moment was,
born from the uplift of power
that sank the aircraft

carriers of the rising sun,
bombed the libraries and concert halls
of men who murdered the Jews of Europe
and stacked their skulls in the world's imagination.

Our dream was American
as baseball, as war,
brief as a song on top-forty.

So what if we never found her?
We three amigos steering her
down the Great Highway in our dreams
—that's as real as anything.

The blue sky
radiated from our Skylark's chrome,
her V8 engine sang with full-throated ease
as we glided through the years of our manhood
behind the wheel of a song.

Or

Finned or on the wing
Rooted or foot propelled

Dressed to the nines
or Salvation Army free box

Plays well with others
or out there on your own

Sent from God
or look what the cat dragged in

Barbered and nails done
or picking fleas from your scalp

Golden slippers
or sneakers patched with duct tape

5G
or two tin cans and a length of string

Hanging on your every word
or shut the fuck up

Clueless
or elementary my dear Watson

The wind at your back
or ain't nothing working

Lungs filling with air for your first cry
or refrigerated, a name tag on your big toe.

To Whoever Broke into My Cabin

First thing I noticed when I drove up
was the big window smashed.
I guess that's how you got the bed out.
I've slept on the floor before,
just wish you had left me a blanket.

If you'd stuck around maybe I'd have poured you a drink.
But I was forgetting—you stole my whiskey.
And it can't be on the rocks
because you stole my fridge.
I'd ask you to sit down, but you stole my chairs.

I could sweep up the broken glass
and roll out my prayer rug for us to sit on.
Bought it in the bazaar, when I unrolled it
the cabin became a holy place.
But I almost forgot, you stole that too.

A time like this, I miss my records.
Junior Wells might soothe my soul.
"Somebody done hoodooed the hoodoo man"
would sound good in this empty space.
Did you listen to it before you sold it?

You used my money to score by now?
Feeling all kicked back and mellow?
They tell me the stuff you like gives a man
that loose, warm, got-it-covered,
world's-a-beautiful-place glow.

Let's talk, you bastard.
There's lots of things we could talk about—
Self-respect, or friendship.
We could even talk about who you are,
because I think I know.

A Spy in the House of Pain

Once I show my pass and they let me in,
I order a bowl of chili at the café
inside the outer gate and outside the inner.

For the cooks, it must feel good
to get out of the cell for an hour or two,
light fire under meat,
shake the earthiness of cumin and oregano
into red beans that have soaked all night
while the prison slept.

Maybe I need the chili
for the sound I am about to hear—
metal clanging on metal,
dead-bolt slamming into place—
after I empty my pockets
and hand over my briefcase to be searched
and make my way inside the house of pain.

The racket of imprisonment:
domino players slapping tiles,
smack of a handball hard against the wall,
iron clanging as the muscle men work out.

Ducktailers who walked off the set
of Blackboard Jungle
reappear years later in the Yard, still
slicking back their hair with Brylcreem.
The Nation of Islam meanders, disputing theology,
jailhouse queens parade.

And is that Crazy John over there
in his mirrored aviators
and explosion of hair and Nazi tattoos?

The homeboys and the Aryans, the Black Guerilla Family,
the Latin Kings—
the whole locked-up nation at war with themselves.
And a guard watching from the tower,
finger on the trigger.

Two Fires

Red coals in a campfire,
peppercorns rubbed into steak.
Friends gather with wine and a guitar.
At a distance, the purl
of a river rippling over shoals,
fireflies in the offing.

The second fire?
Dryness in the air, depletedness.
Midday light goes coppery,
then the radio starts buzzing
and you're in your car,
belongings crammed into garbage bags,
your photo albums and your meds,
the dog on the backseat whining.

Can it be true what they say in the Bible?
Man springs up like grass
that is cut down and thrown into the fire,
but the earth endures forever?

Everything becomes a wick—
Doug firs incinerating,
combustion half a mile high,
fire making weather of its own,
pyrocumulus setting off
lightning strikes.

A pillar of fire like something in the Torah.
Another town goes up in fury—
Paradise, Blue River, Phoenix—
refrigerators, propane tanks, cars
exploding—fire casting embers ten miles
in advance of the blaze.

Fire engendering new words:
firenados supercells fire-whirls
strong enough to
pick a truck up
and spin it around above the ground
then drop it back to earth.

That campfire, that gathering of friends,
those steaks, that bottle of wine, those fireflies,
that river running between its banks—
seem an illusion from an earlier world.

Coyotes trot out of the woods,
ready to tangle with pets.
Rattlesnakes migrate over county lines,
bears come around hungry and aggressive.

What are the trees saying among themselves
down there in the commonwealth of roots?

Uncle

"Uncle," the boy said to me
in the language of his country,
using the word for father's brother,
and asked me the way to the bazaar.
I was a foreigner,
standing by the ferry landing
    looking out to sea.

He was a boy from the villages, I guessed,
neither poor nor not poor,
wearing a soccer shirt,
his cap turned sideways.
I gave him directions, pointed the way,
my accent good enough at least
    to be understood.

Moments before, I had been a foreigner,
now something had changed.
I was a foreigner and not a foreigner.
I was a relative, a more or less
kindly man of a certain age—
ready to be relied upon a member
    of the family, an uncle.

The Self

Sultan Beyazit sprang from a line of warriors,
men who could shoot an arrow
through a sheet of metal four inches thick.
Men who could leap from one horse
to another at a gallop,
and hit with the javelin a raven
perched atop a distant minaret.

Not Beyazit. His was a life of prayer and fasting.
Seven years he never tasted meat.
But appetite being what it is—
that force within, that craving so urgent
it almost becomes our self—

one day this saintly man
developed a craving for *paça.*
He ordered the royal cook to prepare a dish
of the sheep's feet,
well seasoned with garlic and vinegar.
The chef kissed his fingertips
when he presented the dish at the Sultan's table.

Feeling the appetite rising within him,
Beyazit said to it,
Have the paça,
leave my body, go and enjoy—
whereupon a living creature was seen to issue forth
from the Sultan's mouth, and it drank of the juices
in the dish, then tried to return whence it came.
Beyazit raised his hand and stopped
the creature from entering his mouth,
and it fell to the ground.

Beyazit ordered his pages,
Beat it, punish it,
and they kicked it to death on the ground.

The dead thing was prayed over by the imams
and buried in a small tomb on the palace grounds.
Thus after his death it was said that Beyazit
was the only man to die twice and twice be buried.

When the Chinese Came to Our Village

Latoe, Western Tibet

I.

When the Chinese came to our village
they went from house to house
looking for anything old, anything
made from precious metal, any precious stones,
the things each family was proudest of.
Statues of Buddha they melted down for the silver.
My grandmother had a silk dress—
they made her take it off and give it to a Chinese lady.

"Everything belongs to the people," they said,
        and took our chickens.
The cow we kept for milk
bellowed and rolled her eyes
    and tugged on the rope
  as they dragged her down the path.

We were in the fields by dawn
and walked home by lantern light.
At the end of the year
a ration of grain was doled out to each family.
You earned stars that determined how much you got.
I remember I got half a star.

2.

Our only freedom was in the mountains.
My grandfather would take me with him
to herd sheep in the high country pastures.
The wind slammed against you with the strength
of a strong man, but we milked the sheep
and made yogurt, an unimaginable luxury.
We threw rocks at the eagles that circled,

and lit fires at night
to keep wolves from snatching the lambs.
These were enemies we could understand.

2.

Night Train to Memphis

Going Down Slow

The cut and carve of the Gibson guitar
took me back down there—
bottleneck over steel strings
saying *I'm coming on home,*
scuffed Fender amp distorting the high notes

like a 40-watt bulb blinking off and on
in a one-room shack. Out in the road
the Devil was down on his knees shooting dice.
A rattlesnake lay in the dust
in the Mount Zion burying ground

caught in its death-writhe, skin crinkly as cellophane,
whitened ribs open to heaven
while the churchiness of the Hammond B3
sanctified the danger-prone sky.
saying *Somebody call my mother,*
tell her the shape I'm in.

In the early morning rain
I saw a long box strapped with rope
on a railroad platform in Memphis,
waiting for the southbound train.

River Town

My city came with its own tangle of meanings,
bars and backseats where I
lost my innocence avidly,
gardenias, pure intoxication
when worn by the girl I was in love with.

Real and mythical at once,
noisy and demotic
or "quiet and pure as a peach"
as Adam Zagajewski said,
writing of someplace I've never been.

Memphis was all of that to me—
a river town with a name strangely Egyptian
but with pool halls and Masonic temples Alexandria
could never have imagined.
Cotilions and columned
Taras built on cotton and bondage,
hacked out of a wilderness primeval and Mississippian
with axes and ruthlessness
and labor off the slave ship.

A gypsy woman on Beale Street
told your fortune for twenty-five cents,
two boys under a sweetgum tree
played mumbledy-peg with a pocket knife
while a dog looks on.

That gypsy woman, that pocket
knife, statues in the park,
the weeds growing up through cracks in the concrete,
percussion of a basketball on city sidewalks.
In the breeze, hickory smoke and pig.
Listen to Phineas Newborn playing the Memphis Blues.

That's what I'm talking about—
the walk, the weary of it, and then
like church bells from blocks away,
a voice rises up singing.

While someone stood over an ironing board
pressing starch into a shirt
and someone had his head under the hood
of a V8 Ford
and someone else was checking a patient's blood pressure
or selling a piece of real estate,

someone else a few streets away
was composing a melody,
brushing one color next to another,
putting words together to see what they might mean.
I was one of those, I still am.

Beale Street and the Peabody Hotel

A pint of moonshine or a pint
of freshly picked strawberries.
A nickel bag of reefer, sassafras root
for your winter cough. A mojo hand, a black cat bone—
you could buy it all on Beale Street.
The air was funky with catfish frying.
A gypsy woman would read your palm for a dime.
Shuffle in brogans or strutting in wingtip shoes,
Saturday was sinful with the blues
and love for sale when the sun went down.

At the Peabody two streets over,
collars unbuttoned and toddies were poured
in the cool of the day, now that the crop
was sold and on its way downriver.
The talk was of duck hunting and Ole Miss
football and women and the price of cotton.
The planters' ladies and their Julias and Virginias
took their high heels off and undressed
and slipped into frocks they had bought that afternoon.
Prime rib for dinner, and in the evening, swing and sway.

Sunday morning was Let My People Go
or Book of Common Prayer. Same gospel, two ways
of telling it. At the foot of Beale the Mississippi
held its tongue, and flowed as it had since the days
when God and the glacier split the land in two.

Rejoicement for Brother Ray

It's a red dirt road,
  it's a one room country shack.
It's muddy water on baptism Sunday.
It's catfish skinned with a pocket knife.

It's a 40-watt bulb swinging from a
          cord on the ceiling,
three fingers picking out a riff
    on the cracked keys of a church piano.

It's straight up don't always cut it.
It's a girl with a red dress on
    walking the highway at night.
It's a handful of crumpled dollar bills,
          a Greyhound bus,
       red taillights in the rain.

It's get outta my yard
    and don't come back.
It's a drumstick ringing silver
     on cracked cymbals.

It's keeping watch by a sickbed,
        the river rising.
It's a woman weeping as she
hangs out the wash.

It's a choir of empty bottles
         hanging in a spirit tree,
       chiming with the wind.

Sweeping

1.

A woman squatting, with dusty heels,
 looks up into the blue
  sky stretched overhead.

Toward both horizons, east and west
beyond her yard,
 rows of cotton plants extend.

This morning of the world
 she sweeps parallel lines into the dirt,
humming an introspective tune.

2.

Hear the crisp Shhhh! of sweeping—
 that perfectly mindless
  quick sibilant rasp.

There was always dirt.
But the desire for order,
how many lifetimes ago did that emerge,
 broomstraw over bare soil or sand—

in what camp or cave,
 what border town on the outskirts of empire?

3.

At first they must have bundled
twigs, rushes, reeds together—
our forebears—,
bound them with strips of hide.
Someone would know, not me.
But do you remember
when we were children in Memphis
around the time of the two wars in Europe—
and the country people would come to town
with their mules and wagons
calling out *Watermelon!* and *Red ripe tomatoes!*

and selling little bundles of sassafras roots?

And the blind men too,
soft-fleshed, shuffling, shirts poorly tucked in,
peddling the brooms they made.

I stared unabashed into their blue moon eyes,
not able to ponder the connection
between those two essentials—
a skill for the unprotected,

and our fight against the dust we inhabit.
The fight we always lose.

Threads

When I say he was a presence
in the house where I grew up,
I don't mean as a ghost. My dead
grandfather would have had, I think,
too much tact to return
after the dirt had been shoveled, the limousines
parked, the black clothes folded and put away.
Still, his spirit inhabited our house.

He was born the last year of the war
in Tennessee, and he died
the last year of the war in France,
burning up with influenza the troops
brought back from the trenches.
When the Baptist preacher came to his bedside
to pray for him, Grandfather asked him would he
please go out and get him a cold bottle of beer.

Grandfather died with his reserve intact.
How little I know of the man!
I touch, wondering, the keys he left
among his things, their antiquated
edges still sharp to the touch:
lockbox, cash drawer, strongbox,
office door and locks unknown—
keys to nothing.

When I was seventeen I found
in the back of the attic
his silk frayed smoking jacket, his chesterfield
coat with those velvet lapels. I wore
his clothes until
I wore them out, feeling his spirit
breathe through the threads. Here's his gold
watch on my table. I keep it wound.

Daddy's Hands

I drove all night to get there
but I got there too late.
When I made the undertaker open the coffin,
there my father lay,
hands folded across his chest.

I hadn't noticed before
how ridged his nails were.
Even in death
his hands looked intent and purposeful.

In his woodshop on Saturdays
Daddy thought with his hands—
angling a design on the jigsaw,
marking inches off on a board.

He handled wood like I imagine Dürer did
when he cut lines into a block of applewood
for one of his prints,
and then there's a horse running, or a king
or a rabbit, or the vacant eyes
of death on a starveling apocalyptic horse.

As a boy I'd stand beside him, barely able to see
over the top of the workbench, asking my questions.
How old would I have to be to drive the car?
When would he let me shoot the .22?
Half listening, intent on the task at hand,
"All in good time," he would say.
"All in good time."

As I looked down at him
that morning I speak of,
the questions I asked were different—
questions no one but the dead could answer.

We Say Goodbye

in memoriam Helen Pringle Gibbs
1941-2023

These names of ours—chiseled
as they might be
into granite or marble,
important to a handful of souls,
inconsequential otherwise
among the atoms in the galaxies—
resist rain and snow half a century or more,
then erode and become unreadable.

When I think of Helen I see a temple—
neoclassical, something from Greece, something of us.
White columns vertical and pristine,
a palmetto tree growing to one side
shaggy and unregulated.

That geometry, and her departure from it,
that was Helen,
amusement animating the corners of her mouth
before she unleashed a bilingual pun,
a well-considered jab,
or a flurry of badinage.

How many impulses
came together to make her who she was?
Books and lessons, learning of all sorts,
conjugations, which fork to use,
words to say and not to say.
Then love, lace, a husband and children,
and what was it St. Teresa of Avila said?
"God dwells among the pots and pans."

Memory leaps
and there she is in a hotel lobby in Rome
reading poetry from a paperback,
her little girl at her feet drawing a picture,
her little boy building something with blocks.
"Love calls us to the things of this world,"
she reads aloud.
The children look up for a moment, then
go back to what they were doing.

This afternoon that spark
of intelligence, decency and good sense,
infinitesimal inside the darkness we inhabit,
becomes a clutch of ashes
scattered by a living human hand
onto fast-moving water.

Restless

"Run the red light."
—last words of Alex Chilton

In back of where you stand
between a magnolia and a water oak
the little street unravels south,
wavery in the heat.

If you followed it
over the tracks, their steel rails
incandescent with smokestack
lightning off the midnight train

into an unfamiliarity of mismatched houses,
washing machines on porches,
air peppery and bloodshot,
Chevrolets with their hoods raised,
baseball on the radio,
a pawn shop with a guitar in the window,
revival tent in a vacant lot,
you'd still know where you were.

Keep going back
to where the sky blinks open
blue and unimpeded
from the river to the trees—
Corinthian columns rotting,
sassafras and jungling muscadine,
wisteria colonizing a tennis court.

This is the sky you know,
the air you breathe.
That guitar from the pawn shop
is the one you play.

This is who you are.
Why would you want to leave?

The Ends of the Earth

The wind shears through hardwoods,
then rain brings down the leaves

here, eight thousand miles east of
their archipelago of service,
maplike now in its remoteness.

Woodsmoke censes the air
in the hermitage they have made for themselves.
A tin roof snugs it in.

And is that a cricket singing?

The moorings of a life
tighten, creak and hold.
Hearth fires burning the dead growth of the forest
enact a sacrament.

A church bell back there
resonates over emerald rice fields,
waterfalls and terraced mountainsides
and the boars'-teeth-necklaced tribesmen
they lived among:

pipe-smoking heads of families and their wives,
brown-footed sons who herd the pigs,
pointy-breasted daughters.

Drawn by the Sunday bell
into a sanctuary of tiled coolness,
they look up into rafters
where birds of astonishing colors
sing and raise their young.

Those dearly beloved, barefooted,
tattooed communicants,
   partakers of the body and blood,
when they come to church to pray,
      stack their spears by the door.

Placing the Roses on Her Grave

Placing the roses on her grave
was a gesture of little note
in the life of the city
that islanded the graveyard and its church
where the wedding had been enacted
with lace and whiteness and vows.

The sexton unlocked the iron gate
and let me in,
then shut it behind me
when I walked back into the present tense.
Draft horses conveyed carriages of tourists
over the cobblestones
and tour guides with unlocal accents
narrated a history they could not understand.

Only the moist night had not changed,
salt and sweet off marsh and ocean.

Sixty years between the wedding
and these roses in the dust of her grave.
We kissed, ate dinners off the wedding china,
slept in beds.

My Grandmother Told Me

Find you a place where the trees grow tall,
        where bells tell the hours,
where woodsmoke sharpens the air
      when the year starts to turn.

A place you can sit in a pew
      and hear the ancient words intoned.

      Build you a porch, granny said,
where your dog can lie and dream beside your chair.
          Get a patch of mint growing
      underneath where the faucet drips.

Let there be lightning bugs on summer evenings
       so you can sit out with whiskey
and watch those winged rovers etch their
           fire-paths and courtship journeys.

And the lightning itself, the old lady said. Take time
             to let it thrill you—lightning,
                   and the low knuckling rumble
of thunder from the other side of the mountain.

In the long unfathomable nights
              let the rain on your rooftop lay its long
fingers on your sleep, and take the hurt away
           from what surrounds us.

Night Train to Memphis

Slicks of rain
streak the moving window of my train.
My trunk's in the baggage car
and I'm counting the passing stations
like beads on a rosary.

Nightfall along the Blue Ridge,
the locomotive sending a voice
down valleys so lonely,
only the deer lift up their heads to listen.

A lady in a black dress
sits by herself next to the window,
reading the letters of St. Paul to the Corinthians.

Somebody's got a guitar, and a bottle of bourbon.
Here come the old songs.

Then it's dawn—
wisteria pale on a hillside with cedars—
and I hear a bell.
It must be Sunday, cars cluster in the rain
under the modest spire of the Cumberland
Presbyterians, quarried stone of the Methodists,
white columns of the Chamber of Commerce Baptists.
And up on surly hillsides
the meeting houses of the snake handlers,
their music cranked up too loud for the Sabbath.

If Memphis were Jerusalem I'd be a Jew.
But I'm not.
I'm an equivocal Anglican,
snake handler and shouter, backslid Baptist,
Old Believer and apostate.

If I could catechize like St. Paul
and name, like him, three things abiding,
they might be
faithlessness, unkindness,
and the hope that love holds out.

Every trip home
is a pilgrimage into the self.
What other way is there
to find out who you are?
I need to follow my footsteps backwards,
bewildered and astonished
into my childhood—
so I can enter the sanctuary of becoming.

You sinners & heretics,
backsliders, shouters, promise breakers,
lovers with hearts as cold
as the rain on Main Street,
pray for me as I step down off the train.

3.

"Things that seem whole and immutable are only the remnants of a much larger vanishing."
—Antonio Muñoz Molina

"All the rivers run into the sea. Yet the sea is not full."
—Ecclesiastes I:7

How to Get Here

Drive up past the mailboxes
and chimneys of the settlement,
past a one-eyed
palomino grazing a field that looks off
into galaxies.

You'll find me surrounded by
my dials and numbers,
my trees and sails.

Gary said *Lay down these words*
before your mind like rocks
placed solid, by hands.
But nothing feels solid anymore.

Overhead a hawk glides,
bringer of omens,
spirit-sailor, nameless.
I'm peregrine too, perched
at the top of this broken road.

Solstice

A breath indrawn
opens the afternoon.
A hawk buoyed by thermals
peers down
over these ridges and valleys.

How still the day is
this late in June.
With a word to no one,
a leaf exhales.

There goes the I'm-all-alone
call of a dove.
The chickens, their day's work done,
speak their small syllables, then
pomp-and-circumstance toward their perches.

Not a dog barks, not an engine
turns over. Not a nail is hammered,
not a match is struck
or a string plucked.
Not a shirt is hung on a line.

Just you and me up here at the end
of the road at the end of the day.
A big moth flutters
from under the overhang.
Everyone has gone away.

Emblems

A sailing ship thirteen inches high
from the planking of its deck
to the top of the mainsail.
Next to the ship, a bronze dolphin
coasting on its muscles.

A Japanese bowl
glazed green, color
of remote seas,
lives on this table too,
the closest thing I have to an altar.

When the dolphin
leaps and the bowl
fills, and when
the ship
slips harbor

I swing onboard,
hearing the music of its taut-strung lines
as wind fills the sails
and dailiness
is left behind in port.

Umami

Steam from soba boiling
  has gone to my head.
My kitchen's a rain forest,
the roof of my mouth-cave darkens.
As I cook, I enter under dripping trees
   and forage for shitake
among leaves rotting under slow rain.

Back in the forest, barrels
    of anchovies
        mellow under lantern light.
Moss grows over the barrels.
            Garlic I already had, and now
exhalations of oysters, tamari, seaweed
float with the resonance of a struck gong
over broth the noodles have tinctured.

As you dip in your spoon,
  I watch like a mother
      at her daughter's
     cello recital.

Waterborne

Rain rivering the gutters,
arpeggios falling through oak leaves,
witching a storm from across the ocean
    out of a channel
threaded with leviathans

breaching the swells with joy,
submerging deep and unfathomable,
their muscles a mystery,
    songlines uncharted,
their intervals unknown.

Somebody loan me a coin—
I have a wish to make,
a petition to enter.
  I need to pay the boatman
to row me across.

Lead me to that well I've heard about.
Let me ladle up a cupful
from the fountain where prayers
float like petals on the brimming tide.
  I've got to take off my shoes
and wash the unworthiness from my feet.

Fishing Downstream

We're fishing our way downstream,
my friend and I,
watching the ways of the water as we drift,
the trees' darkness outlined against
the day's last brilliance.

A white moth
flutters from the trees,
lands on the river,
and a big trout slurps him up.

A whirl of wind
whips the tops of the larches
and now I'm
up above where my backcast
loops and flexes.
A nighthawk guides me.

The moon's up here with us,
the beggar they see from the
other side of the world
with a load of kindling
on his back,
outlined against the disk of silver.

Nighthawk, what's it like
to be aloft always,
not to drift as James and I do
on the ribbon of liquid
that threads its way through the forest?

Your house is fashioned of air,
the larches are your wainscoting, the moon
transits while you hunt.

Higher still, the stars.

All of us are in transit.
The moth has the briefest moment,
then the trout, and the nighthawk,
then James and me.

Then what, the trees?
Then the river, the moon,
then the mortal stars.

One Night in Galilee

We were looking to bed down for the night,
get the flock together safe and the dogs
keeping watch. Rain had started to fall.

Then the music came:
commanding and lofty,
but warm-hearted and human too.
It reached out and
found us where we lay.

Fear not, a voice said.
And out of the voice emerged a figure.
He looked like a man
but we knew he wasn't.

How could we welcome such a one?
Offer him goats' milk to drink?
Find a place for him in our tent,
smelling as it did of tallow and long days
handling animals,
on the move for months?

Before we could make up our minds,
the air came alive with angels' wings—
air that a moment before had been
heavy with mud-mist and sheep funk.

The sound of their wings
was a river at flood-tide.
Their plumage dazzled—
this choir half glimpsed
singing their message
of peace on Earth,
a royal family in a stable,
a baby who would be a king.

And when they had gone away
into heaven,
we looked at each other dumbstruck.
It was night again,
the dogs hung close and held their tongues.
Then someone said,
Let us go and see.

The Household of the Word

In response to" My Faithful Mother Tongue"
by Czeslaw Miłosz

How would the lords and ladies
of the air be swifted to their wedding feasts and cotilions
among the trees, without your carriage
    fairy-springed and spirited?

And the corpses of young men cut down by cannon fire
on bloody slopes—by what conveyance could we
bear to see them trundled into mass graves if not
        for the Anglo-Saxon edge

of your pick and spade, if not in the hard-hammered
cart of your construction—boards rough cut,
square nailed, bumping over stones fit to bear
            the chronicles of grief?

The threadbare impulses of mothers' hearts,
those voiceless chambers, how could they hope
to rise to the foot of the throne except in the fabric
          of your articulation?

Maybe there's a place for me in your household,
I said to myself back then, though I was tongue-tied
among the talkers and rhymers
          and tellers of tales

and dusty hermits who came down
from their caves to carouse at your table.

Listen!
If I didn't have your house to live in,
    where else would I have lived?

A Dream of My Life

I dreamed I lived in a house where shapers
of masterworks, craftsmen
with radiance in their fingertips
unrolled panoramas across my worktable,
transfigured my walls into earthly paradise,
then sat with me in that halo
drinking demitasses of fire,
bargaining high-spiritedly,
toasting art and friendship.

Yet here was my flaw:
I was a householder of means, wainscoted
and waistcoated, mixing a bowl of punch for my guests,
and at the same time a crosseyed
bootlegger spiking the bowl
with kerosene.
A Raskolnikov lurking consumptively,
in the pocket of my jacket
a pamphlet by Lenin.

There was a woman in my dream
I might have saved through love
or so it seemed to me,
if only my heart were a better heart.

An old woman
I might have let teach me
and bring fulfilment to her years.

But who could teach me anything?

What brought me to lock the door behind me,
toss the golden key to that house
up into the sun,

where it flashes
and disappears without a splash
in the out-going tide?

The Gardener

The past is a foreign country; they do things differently there.
—L.P. Hartley

While drums pounded and cymbals
Drove men mad and bronze siege cannon
Pulverized walls built to last till the day
Of judgment, Fatih Mehmet—Shadow and Spirit of God
Among men, Monarch of the Terrestrial Orb,
Lord and Master of the Three Worlds—
Commanded music to be played in his tent,
Herodotus was read to him by candlelight in Greek,
The poems of Rumi and Hafez recited in Persian.

His hobby, his leisure, his relaxation, this Lord
Of Two Continents and Two Seas, was gardening.
Finding one day that one of his prized cucumbers
Was missing from the vine, and suspecting his head gardener,
He seized the man, drew from his belt a dagger
Ornamented with rubies, and ripped the man's belly open.
Chunks of cucumber, half-digested, tumbled out
Mixed with the dark blood of the gardener's entrails.
Students of human nature, help me take this in.

The Messenger

The sheep moved like a muddy cloud
over the hills and red-dirt arroyos.
We ranged footloose alongside,
guiding the flock,
our dogs alert for wolves.
Juanito carried a Winchester carbine.

The others make allowances
for the things I see,
knowing I was the one who was sent away
to be imprinted with the wisdom from books,
to read the flight of birds,
learn to cypher, understand spells,
get information from the crows.

I had walked a mile from camp
into the foothills of the Sangre de Cristos.
That's when it happened—
the sky was a staircase
lighted as if with fireflies,
steps descending.
It was on these stairs
that the messenger came down.

His appearance was that of a man,
but I knew he was other.

The feathers that swirled around him
were of no bird that nests in the trees around here.
His mouth opened like the
beak of the eagle.

His words were of the court,
but he spoke them
with the tenderness of a grandmother.

Let me see if I can translate:

Some hunt, he said.
Some keep watch over the flocks.
This is not who you are.
Speak in the language of owls, he said.
Translate the rivered turnings of serpents
into words all of us can understand.

Who knows what to make of these messages?
I built a fire of mesquite
where the messenger had stood
and turned the air to incense.

We Kept a Room for Him

We kept a room for him, fire laid,
the bed made up.
He was a kinsman of my father's
and he'd stop with us
when he came in off the desert.
The children crowded round
and begged to handle his sword,
honed sharp for killing,
so heavy I could hardly lift it.
I'd give his sandals to the servant girl to clean
and rub sheep's oil into.

His bodyguards and archers positioned themselves
in the hills around.
They knew how to keep out of sight.
The kitchen would send food to them.

When he was bathed and rested, dressed in a fresh robe,
he'd sit and talk
over a bowl of my wife's soup.
The young ones would be after him
to tell about his travels.

He told us of a horse with wings—
a fabulous beast with a woman's face
and the tail of a peacock
that flew him above the seven heavens.
Comets roared by, galaxies
were born and died.

We learned from him of a cave
above the Abyss of Chaos
where the voices of the dead were heard,
and liquid syllables flowed
from the rivers of Paradise.

One night,
after we'd talked to some late hour,
he gave his compliments all round
and was about to rise and retire.
I had lighted a lamp for him to carry up with him.
Looking down at the cat stretched out on his cloak
and purring in her sleep,
he asked my daughter for scissors
and then he cut around the
cloth he was sitting on,
so as not to disturb the cat.

Pilgrims come to the city now
but not to our house.
We keep the square of cloth he cut out
for ourselves, tied with green ribbon
in a chest underneath the stairs.

I Left the Encampment Early

A high wind agitated the pines
but the yurt bore the brunt of it
with barely a shrug of its roofpoles.
I packed with care, and left the encampment early.
A raven flew over, cawing,
let the camp dogs bark all they will.

My feet crunched the pine needles of the road out,
loosening tendons arthritic,
my legs not strong.

I choose my steps carefully, in the way of age.

Don't Disappear

I call to him and say come back,
don't disappear.
But he's switchbacks ahead of me,
old uncle, grizzled enigma,
still climbing.

When he stops to rest
he hollows out a place for himself
among stones along the trail.
I find the charred signs of his campfires.

I think he must hear, in the sleepless dog-howling
mosquito-aggravated nights,
the low notes of an abandoned harmony
that keeps him going

over wind-bothered uplands.
His stopping places
are deconsecrated chime-haunted
ruins from a religion that disappeared traceless—
frescoes of saints with their eyes scratched out,
acres of forgetfulness,
the countryside deforested,
wisps of fog hanging among the pines
like shredded prayer flags.

I call to him and say come home uncle,
grandpa, father.
But I can't reach him.
His face dissolves like a cloud.

Who Will Tell the Bees?

The Queen is dead. Who will tell the bees?
The scarlet and black, the royal blue
and Navy blue
have trooped past—boots
striking the pavement,
bells echoing on stone,
roses softly tossed onto the passing hearse.

Who will tell the Queen's bees her ponies
feel the same as they do,
and the mournful, low-slung dogs
that walked with her?

Who will lift the sable cloths off their hives
and tell the bees
the ceremony of never-endingness
has been fulfilled?
Something out of the deep remove,
something as patterned as their honeycombs,
the halo around the crown,
the authority inside a diamond,
has been carried forward.

Maybe they already knew.
My eyes left the screen and
entered a waking dream
where the bees swarmed Westminster
and rose between Hawksmoor's towers
into the vaulted arches of stone.
It was so pure a reckoning,
the swarm of their perfection
matched the marble diamonds
of the abbey's floor.
Only the plaint of the royal piper
could comfort them.

Where Did They Go

The gypsies playing jazz
in the piazza, dark water lapping on stone
catching tongues of moonlight.
Frascati brimmed in our glasses,
the pasta on our plates had the sea in it,
    the briny Adriatic.

Where did they go? The scarf you wore,
with its William Morris design.
The words and non-words
of our *lessico famigliare.*
Our boldness. The way we had
    with each other.

We sailed out at night toward the islands
on that wheezy Greek freighter,
warm under tartans in our deck chairs.
In the vastness above us the constellations
wheeled, each with its own
    story to tell.

Canzona di Ringraziamento

Beethoven,
string quartet number 15 in A Minor,
Opus 132

for Garrett Hongo

There's a key for every decade of our life,
and A Minor's the key for my ninth.

It's getting dark,
and outside the concert hall in Budapest
a thunderstorm blows.
Inside, the houselights decline
and the cellist agitates the low string
with his horsehair bow

like a long spoon muddling spirits
the color of mahogany in a glass.
People in the balconies feel the march
of thunder outside.
A man in evening dress in one of the stalls
takes out a gold watch and looks at it
and wonders, like me, what it means to die.

Look for a place above sorrow,
the cello sings.
The viola finds a channel
under the brilliance of the violins,
whose strings touch every nerve.
Find forgiveness for your transgressions,
the viola tells me.
Feel tenderness even toward yourself.

A Minor's the key of ripeness.
You can feel it in the hall
above the thunder *appassionato.*

A cortège paces in the adagio.
And yet Beethoven calls his third movement *canzona di ringraziamento,* a song of gratitude.
Give thanks
for this music that says no matter what,
we're not done yet.

Acknowledgments

I am grateful to the editors of the following journals, where some of these poems originally appeared:

American Journal of Poetry: "Or"
Asheville Poetry Review: "Waterborne" & "When Did It Begin?"
Bear River Review: "The Feast of the Hungry," "The Household of the Word," and "The Mission"
Beloit Poetry Journal: "Solstice"
Best of Delmarva Review: "Canzona di Ringraziamento"
Birmingham Poetry Review: "Beale Street and the Peabody Hotel," "The Messenger" "Night Train to Memphis," "The Self," & "A Spy in the House of Pain"
Delmarva Review: "Canzona di Ringraziamento" & "Daddy's Hands"
Fiddlehead: "How to Get Here"
First Things: "The Ends of the Earth" & "The Gardener"
Gavialidae: "Don't Disappear," "The Mission," "Sweeping," "Two Libraries" & "Where Did They Go?"
Great River Review: "Threads"
Harvard Review: "Two Fires"
Hudson Review: "A Dream of My Life" & "The Household of the Word"
Image Journal: "One Night in Galilee"
Literary Imagination: "Going Down Slow" & "Fishing Downstream"
The New Criterion: "The Feast of the Hungry"
Plume Poetry Journal: "When the Chinese Came to Our Village"
Poetry Northwest: "Emblems"
Salmagundi: "How I Learned," "Placing the Roses on Her Grave," "Restless," "Skylark" & "To Whoever Broke into My Cabin"
Southern Poetry Review: "I Left the Encampment Early"
Southern Review: "We Kept a Room for Him"
Swing: "Who Will Tell the Bees?"
Wonderlust: "Autumn Comes to Hamakua" & "River Town"

At first, "To Whoever Broke Into My Cabin" owed almost everything to Steve Scafidi's poem, "To Whoever Set Fire to My Truck." It started out as a pastiche of Steve's poem. Then it became my own.

"When the Chinese Came to Our Village" is an adaptation of stories told me by my friend Dawa Myers, who lived through and survived the brutal repression inflicted on the Tibetan people during the Chinese conquest of their country.

I told the story recounted in "The Self" in prose in my 2012 book, *Istanbul: City of Forgetting and Remembering.* "The Self" draws heavily on the account of the Ottoman Sultan Beyazit II given in Evliya Çelebi's 17th-century chronicle called *Seyahatname.*

"Going Down Slow" riffs on the song of the same name written by St. Louis Jimmy Oden and sung by Howlin' Wolf, Aretha Franklin, and many other great singers. "Night Train to Memphis" is the name of a song written by Beasley Smith, Owen Bradley, and Marvin Hughes, and recorded in 1942 by Roy Acuff.

Richard Tillinghast's latest book, *Blue If Only I Could Tell You,* won the 2022 White Pine Press Poetry Prize. *Night Train to Memphis* is his fourteenth poetry collection, in addition to five books of creative nonfiction. His poems have appeared in the *American Poetry Review, The Atlantic, The New Yorker, Paris Review, The New Republic, The Best American Poetry* and elsewhere. He is recipient of the Amy Lowell Traveling Poetry Scholarship as well as grants from the Guggenheim Foundation, the National Endowment for the Arts, and the National Endowment for the Humanities. Richard currently lives in Hawaii and spends his summers in Tennessee.